D0745194

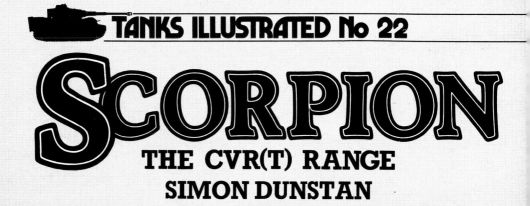

TANKS ILLUSTRATED No 22

SCORPION

THE CVR(T) RANGE

SIMON DUNSTAN

ARMS AND ARMOUR PRESS

London   New York   Sydney

Introduction

Published in 1986 by Arms & Armour Press Ltd.,
2–6 Hampstead High Street, London NW3 1QQ.

Distributed in the United States by Sterling
Publishing Co. Inc., 2 Park Avenue, New York,
N.Y.10016.

© Arms & Armour Press Ltd., 1986
All rights reserved. No part of this publication may
be reproduced, stored in a retrieval system, or
transmitted in any form by any means electrical,
mechanical or otherwise, without first seeking the
written permission of the copyright owner.

British Library Cataloguing in Publication Data:
Dunstan, Simon
Scorpion: the CVR(T) Range.—(Tanks illustrated;
v. 22)
1. Armored vehicles, Military—History
I. Title   II. Series
623.74'75   UG446.5

ISBN 0-85368-747-1

Editing, design and artwork by Roger Chesneau.
Typesetting by Typesetters (Birmingham) Ltd.
Printed and bound in Italy
by GEA/GEP in association with
Keats European Ltd., London.

To Bacchus

◄2
1. (Title spread) By using aluminium alloy armour to
achieve light weight, Scorpion has a high power-to-
weight ratio of 25hp/tonne and hence exceptional
mobility. It has a road speed in excess of 50mph,
although it is supposedly restricted to 40mph for
peacetime training. Acceleration from 0 to 30mph in
16 seconds is possible.
2. In October 1967 Alvis Ltd. of Coventry was
awarded a development contract to build seventeen
prototypes of Scorpion, the first of which was
completed in January 1969. The prototypes were
built by mid-1970 and extensive trials were conducted both at home and abroad, from Queensland to
Norway. The Scorpion was accepted for service with
the British Army in May 1970.

In the late 1950s consideration was given to the replacement of the
Saladin and Ferret wheeled armoured cars following a General Staff
Target for an air-portable armoured reconnaissance vehicle with
improved firepower and mobility. At the time there were conflicting
opinions as to whether the requirement could best be met by a vehicle
on wheels or tracks, and as a result of studies undertaken at the
Fighting Vehicles Research and Development Establishment (now
the Royal Armament Research and Development Establishment) at
Chertsey, it was decided in 1964 to develop two families of vehicles to
fulfil the roles envisaged for the Armoured Vehicle Reconnaissance
(AVR). These emerged as the Combat Vehicle Reconnaissance
(Tracked) Scorpion range and the Combat Vehicle Reconnaissance
(Wheeled) Fox armoured cars, which share the same Jaguar engine
and major automotive assemblies for ease of maintenance and
training.

The tracked design was deemed essential because of its superior
cross-country mobility (which had to match that of the Main Battle
Tanks and Armoured Personnel Carriers employed in North-West
Europe), whereas the wheeled variant had a vital role to play in
operations where movement across country was less important (for
example, protecting lines of communication and carrying out internal
security tasks). The first test rig, known as the TV15000, was
constructed of aluminium armour with a hydropneumatic suspension
and was powered by the Rolls-Royce B60 engine of the Ferret. After
trials of various configurations, a contract for seventeen prototypes of
the tracked version was awarded the following year to Alvis Ltd. of
Coventry, which at the time was manufacturing the FV600 series of 6
× 6 armoured vehicles, the Saladin and Saracen; similarly, a contract
for fifteen prototypes of the wheeled variant was awarded to the
Daimler Co. of Coventry, which was then producing the FV700 range
of Ferret armoured cars.

Over 3,300 of the Scorpion series have been built, and the design
has enjoyed considerable export success. It is in service with the
armies of Belgium, Brunei, Honduras, Iran, Ireland, Kuwait,
Malaysia, New Zealand, Nigeria, Oman, the Philippines, Tanzania,
Thailand, the United Arab Emirates and the United Kingdom (both
with the Army and the Royal Air Force). It has been used in combat
in the Falklands War of 1982, by The Blues and Royals, and during
the Iran–Iraq War. The Fox is employed by the armies of Iran,
Kenya, Malawi, Nigeria, Saudi Arabia and the United Kingdom. On
account of the versatility and soundness of the range, both Scorpion
and Fox have scope for further development, and a number of
variants, beyond the requirements of the British Army, have been
produced for the foreign market: in particular the Stormer family of
vehicles, a mature derivative of the CVR(T) Scorpion, will carry the
basic design concept into the next century.

Unless otherwise credited, all the photographs are included by
courtesy of the MoD Public Relations departments, to whom I extend
my thanks, as I do to Pierre Touzin.

Simon Dunstan

3. Originally designated Armoured Vehicle Reconnaissance (AVR), the design was renamed Combat Vehicle Reconnaissance (Tracked) Fire Support (Scorpion). Scorpion is the lead vehicle of the complete CVR(T) family of vehicles, all of which share the same major automotive components and lower hull structure for ease of maintenance and logistic support.

4. Designed primarily as a reconnaissance vehicle with considerable fire-power, Scorpion mounts a two-man turret to the rear, and in common with all the vehicles in the CVR(T) range, the engine compartment and driver are in the front. This prototype is undergoing trials at the Military Vehicles and Engineering Establishment (MVEE) at Chertsey (now the Royal Armament Research and Development Establishment).

5. The first production Scorpion for the British Army, of an order amounting to some 2,000 CVR(T) vehicles, was delivered in January 1972. User trials had indicated the need for greater stowage space, and large bins were added to the turret and rear hull.

6. The first regiment to be issued with Scorpion was The Blues and Royals, at Windsor in early 1973; the 17th/21st Lancers, at Wolfenbuttel in West Germany, followed later in the year. Here a Scorpion of 'The Death or Glory Boys' takes part in the Exercise 'Glory Hawk'.

▲3   ▼4

5▲   6▼

7. 'Glory Hawk' was conducted in the Harz mountains to the north of the Moselle and was the first major BAOR exercise in which Scorpions participated. Two squadrons of the 14th/20th King's Hussars were also equipped with Scorpions at the time, a pair of which are seen here halted in a field.

8. Scorpions of the 14th/20th fire a salvo of blanks at the conclusion of Exercise 'Glory Hawk'. The 76mm main armament is a lightened version of that fitted to Saladin and fires HESH, HE, canister, illuminating, smoke and practice ammunition. A mixed load of forty rounds is carried.

▲7 ▼8

9. Scorpion is the first British Army vehicle to be made almost entirely of aluminium. The zinc-aluminium-magnesium alloy armour gives ballistic protection over the frontal arc against 14.5mm AP rounds and all-round protection against 7.62mm AP and most shell splinters.
10. REME and American mechanics remove a Scorpion TN15X transmission, derived from the design used in the Chieftain MBT. Scorpion is powered by a derated (190bhp as against 265bhp) Jaguar 4.2 litre XK engine of sports car fame – as are all vehicles in the CVR(T) range – and has a range of 400 miles on roads at a fuel consumption of 4.5 miles per gallon.

9▲   10▼

▲11 ▼12

13▲

11. The J60 engine of a Scorpion undergoes maintenance in the field with the assistance of REME expertise from the Centurion ARV Mk. 2 in the background. For reasons of economy and reliability many of the automotive components are readily available commercial items.

12. A pair of Scorpions, one belonging to the 17th/21st Lancers (left) and the other to the 14th/20th King's Hussars, prepare to race around the famous German Grand Prix motor racing circuit, the Nürnburgring. The result was a dead heat!

13. Well camouflaged with natural vegetation, two Scorpions of the 17th/21st Lancers perform their role of medium reconnaissance during an exercise in West Germany during 1974.

14. A Scorpion forges through the snow at high speed during a NATO exercise in Norway. With its remarkably low ground pressure, less than that of a walking man, Scorpion has excellent flotation and is able to negotiate soft terrain such as bogs, paddy fields and snow with little difficulty.

14▼

▲15 ▼16

15. The suspension of CVR(T) is of the torsion bar type mounted on transverse trailing arms with a maximum vertical wheel movement of 12in, giving a comfortable cross-country ride even at high speeds. For a tracked vehicle, Scorpion is remarkably quiet, with a noise level comparable to a wheeled one of similar weight. (Author)

16. A Scorpion and a Ferret of the 14th/20th King's Hussars motor across a bridge during Exercise 'Red Rat 74'. The vehicles are covered by a 66mm L1A1 anti-tank rocket in the hands of a soldier of the 1st Battalion The Prince of Wales's Own Regiment of Yorkshire.

17. Mounted to the right of the L23A1 76mm main armament is a Rank Precision Industries passive night sight with a dual magnification of 1.6 or 5.8, protected in an armoured housing. The driver also has a passive night-driving periscope.

18. In place of the J60 petrol engine with its inherent fire hazard, Scorpion can be fitted with a six-cylinder turbo-charged Perkins T6.3544 diesel power unit of 200bhp. In trials of the Perkins conducted by the British Army, this vehicle ran for 10,000 miles without failing – a record which compares very favourably with the in-service life of about 5,500 miles for a British Army petrol-engined Scorpion.

21▲

◀22

19. A Scorpion churns up the mud as it moves across country at speed. As befits a reconnaissance vehicle, Scorpion is equipped with numerous vision devices, giving excellent observation even when closed down under NBC conditions. (Author)

20. With just the skull insignia of the 17th/21st Lancers' regimental emblem visible, a Scorpion gunner peers through the vegetation adorning his vehicle. The gunner sits in the right of the turret with the commander (who also acts as loader) to his left.

21. In response to terrorist activity, Scorpions of The Blues and Royals were put on alert to protect Heathrow Airport in 1974. Acting in support of the civil power, the Scorpions were under the control of the police; here a PC 'pounds his beat' on the airport perimeter in an unconventional mode of transport.

22. As are all AFVs of the British Army, Scorpion is equipped with smoke grenade launchers to produce an instant smoke screen. Here smoke grenades fly through the air from the pair of triple discharger cups mounted on the turret front. The smoke screen persists for about 60 seconds, depending on the wind conditions. (Author)

▲23

23. With its turret crew clad in parkas against the cold, a Scorpion ploughs through the snow during an exercise in Norway as part of the NATO Allied Command Europe (ACE) Mobile Force (Land). Scorpion can operate efficiently through an ambient temperature range of −30°C to +50°C.

24. Scorpions of 'C' Squadron, 16th/5th The Queen's Royal Lancers, negotiate a Class 60 Medium Girder Bridge built by engineers of 68 Gurkha Field Squadron in Hong Kong. The Scorpion is ideally suited to the hilly terrain of the British colony and its serves in several such outposts.

▼24

25. Scorpions and Gazelle helicopters parade before Queen Elizabeth II at Sennelager in West Germany on the occasion of Her Majesty's Silver Jubilee in July 1977.
26. Camouflaged in white stripes over its olive green base colour, a Scorpion speeds through the snow during Exercise 'Hardfall' in Norway, 1980. Note the perspex screens protecting the driver and commander against the biting wind.

25▲

26▼

▲27 ▼28

27. A Scorpion motors past another guarding a bridge during an exercise in West Germany. Typically, the crews have added extra stowage bins, as well as spare roadwheels and jerry cans, to carry the creature comforts necessary to make field exercises more bearable. (Pierre Touzin)

28. A Scorpion of the 17th/21st Lancers rushes along a forest track during an exercise in West Germany in 1974. To the left of the 76mm is a coaxially mounted 7.62mm L43A1 machine gun with 3,000 rounds. It can also act as a ranging gun, to conserve main armament ammunition.

29. The Scorpion can ford to a depth of 3ft 6in without pre-paration, and by means of a flotation screen mounted around the top of the hull which can be erected in under five minutes by the crew, the vehicle can negotiate rivers and inland waterways, propelled and steered by its tracks at a speed of 4mph. (Author)

30, 31. Besides the British Army, the Royal Air Force also employs CVR(T), for airfield defence. In November 1981 the RAF Regiment at Catterick took delivery of its first Scorpions from an order of 150 vehicles. Each of the RAF squadrons comprises three 'flights' of Spartan APCs and one of Scorpions, making a total of fifteen Spartans and six Scorpions, together with one Sultan command vehicle and a Samson ARV. Note that this Scorpion is not fitted with a flotation screen around the hull.

29▲

30▲　31▼

▲32

32. A Scorpion of 'A' Squadron, The Blues and Royals, undergoes maintenance during Exercise 'Hardfall' in Norway. Mounted in a 360-degree traverse turret, the 76mm gun has a maximum elevation of 30 degrees and a depression of 10 degrees. The High-Explosive Squash Head (HESH) round is effective out to a range of 3,500m against both armoured targets and field fortifications.

▼33

33. A Grenadier Guardsman protects a civil airliner as a Scorpion of The Blues and Royals patrols the apron of Heathrow airport during Operation 'Trustee' in February 1982 – another exercise to counter possible terrorist acts against the international airport and its travellers.

34. In order to increase realism during field exercises, many AFVs are fitted with Simfire equipment to simulate the full gunnery sequence of engagement. Above the 76mm barrel is a laser Weapon Projector, with detector units mounted around the turret and the radio transmitter/receiver unit, which processes signals passing between engaged and engaging vehicles, on top. On the hull side is the flash generator, which simulates the actual firing with a puff of white smoke. (Author)

35. A Scorpion of 'A' Squadron, The Blues and Royals, leads a 'Big Wheel Ferret' through a town in the mountainous region of Northern Greece during Exercise 'Alexander Express'. The CVR(T) range has a military classification in the FV100 series, Scorpion being FV101.

▲ 36

36. A Scorpion of No. 1 Squadron, RAF Regiment, guards a Harrier site in the West German countryside. No. 1 Squadron is based in West Germany to protect the Harrier Force; the other squadrons are stationed in the UK but in time of war would deploy to West Germany to defend the air bases at Laarbruch, Bruggen and Wildenrath.

37. In its medium reconnaissance role, Scorpion operates in troops or half-troops well forward of the battle area, relaying information about and directing fire against enemy forces. Here a Scorpion operates in conjunction with an FV432 APC.

▼ 37

38. In October 1970 a Memorandum of Understanding was signed by Britain and Belgium for the joint production of CVR(T) to fulfil a requirement of 701 Scorpions and variants for the Belgian Army. These were built at a British Leyland facility at Malines in Belgium from kits made by Alvis, but some components of both British and Belgian vehicles were produced in Belgium. In this photograph, a Scorpion and Scimitar of the Belgian Army pause by the roadside during an exercise in West Germany. (Pierre Touzin)

39. A Scorpion 90 undergoes trials with the British Army to determine the feasibility of a mid-life improvement for the design. Intended primarily for the export market, Scorpion 90 is armed with a 90mm Cockerill gun capable of inflicting severe damage even on MBTs. This version has been purchased by Malaysia, and one example was evaluated in the USMC Light Armored Vehicle (LAV) project. (Author)

▲40 ▼41

40. A prototype Striker Anti-tank Guided Weapon Vehicle shows the armoured launcher bins for five Swingfire missiles raised in the firing position. Striker has been designed as a compact, air-portable tank destroyer capable of knocking out any known AFV out to a range of 4km.

41. While sharing the same main components and lower hull structure as all the other vehicles in the CVR(T) range, Striker is based on the hull of the Spartan APC. It has a crew of three – driver,

commander and missile controller (whose monocular sight has a magnification of ×1 and ×10 and is mounted on the roof adjacent to the commander's cupola).

42. The crew of an FV101 Scorpion catch some sleep on the engine decks during a field exercise. (Author)

43. A section of FV102 Striker ATGW vehicles forms up beside a troop of Chieftain MBTs. (Author)

▲44   ▼45

44. CVR(T) variants, including Sultan, Samaritan, Scimitar and Scorpion, undergo routine maintenance during an exercise on Salisbury Plain. (Author)

45. CVR(T) and CVR(W), Scorpion and Fox, engage tagets on the gunnery ranges at Lulworth in Dorset. (Author)

46. The crew of an FV103 Spartan APC replenish their vehicle in the field. (Author)

46▲

▲47   ▼48

49▲

◄50

47. FV102 Striker Anti-tank Guided Weapon Vehicles move forward during a battle-group exercise. (Author)

48. A crew member of an FV104 Samaritan Armoured Ambulance consults his map before the next phase of an exercise. (Author)

49. The first production FV102 Striker was delivered to the British Army in June 1975 and it entered service with the Royal Artillery anti-tank regiments of BAOR in 1976. ATGW vehicles are now manned by members of the Royal Armoured Corps, with a Guided Weapon Troop per armoured regiment and four troops each of four Strikers per BAOR armoured reconnaissance regiment.

50. A Swingfire is launched from a Striker. The 28kg missile has a HEAT warhead with a minimum/maximum range of 140/4,000m and a time of flight out to 4,000m of 26 seconds. The operator controls the missile in flight by means of a thumb joystick which produces commands that are sent through a wire attached to the missile. (Author)

▲51

51. A troop of Strikers moves through the German town of Benningsen during Exercise 'Steel Trap' in 1979. Besides the five British Aerospace Swingfire missiles in the roof-mounted launcher bins, a further five are carried inside the hull and have to be loaded by one of the crew while outside the vehicle.

52. The missiles can also be launched and controlled by the operator up to 100m from the vehicle. From his detached vantage point he can engage enemy AFVs while Striker remains in a concealed position and is therefore less vulnerable to counter-fire. Striker is in service with both the British and Belgian Armies.

53. Spartan is the Armoured Personnel Carrier of the CVR(T)

range. It was originally intended as a replacement for the Saracen APC and fulfils various roles which require armoured protection for soldiers and equipment on the battlefield. This prototype illustrates the basic hull configuration.

54. The vehicle carries four soldiers in addition to the driver, commander/gunner and section commander (who also acts as the radio operator). The commander serves the 7.62mm machine gun mounted on the cupola with 3,000 rounds of ammunition stowed in the hull. The GPMG can be loaded, cocked, aimed and fired from inside the armoured protection of the vehicle.

▼52

◀55

56▲

◀57

55. Over the top of the troop compartment are two roof hatches which open to either side. Two periscopes are fitted to the left and one to the right of the troop compartment; there is also a vision block in the rear entry door. This early prototype vehicle lacks the commander's cupola common to Spartan and Striker.

56. Spartan entered service with BAOR in 1978. Among its roles, the vehicle carries Royal Artillery teams with Blowpipe/Javelin shoulder-fired surface-to-air missiles for forward air defence. Artillery observers and forward air controllers are transported around the battlefield, as are Royal Engineer assault teams, and it also acts as a missile resupply vehicle for Striker.

57. One of Spartan's principal roles is that of a surveillance vehicle, employing the ZB298 ground radar. This equipment is made by Marconi and can be mounted on the roof or outside on a tripod, with the visual display unit inside the hull. The radar is used for general battlefield surveillance, particularly in conditions of poor visibility or for directing artillery and mortar fire. Night Observation Devices are also carried for this role.

33

▲58   ▼59

34

58. An FV103 Spartan moves across country at speed while closed down. Note the shrouded exhaust pipe along the roof and the GPMG mounted on the commander's cupola which can be remotely operated from inside the vehicle. The flotation screen runs around the top of the hull sides and front. (Author)

59. REME mechanics change the engine of a Spartan APC using a HIAB hydraulic crane mounted on a Stalwart during Exercise 'Royal Reynard' in West Germany in 1979. Note the layout of the power plant, with the transmission and cooling group in the forward compartment, the engine position behind and to the left, and the driver's station at right as viewed.

60. A pair of Spartans drive past a review stand at the conclusion of a field exercise in West Germany. As with all the CVR(T) variants, Spartan has smoke grenade discharger cups mounted forward on the hull. Note the Racal Amplivox 'Helmguard' protective helmets incorporating earphones and boom microphone worn by the crew members.

61. A Spartan kicks up the dust during training at Bovington, the home of the Royal Armoured Corps. With a height of 7ft 5in to the top of the machine gun, Spartan is a compact vehicle. A C-130 Hercules can carry two of them and one can be slung beneath a Chinook HC-1 helicopter. (Author)

60▲ 61▼

35

▲62

▲63   ▼64

62. As a commercial venture Alvis (acquired by United Scientific Holdings in 1981) has proposed the mounting of various missile installations on the Spartan APC. This particular combination is the Euromissile HOT ATGW System on a HAKO mount with two ready-to-fire HOT missiles and a further eight carried inside the hull. Other anti-tank missiles that can be fitted include Hughes TOW and Euromissile Milan systems. (Author)

63. The crew of a Spartan observe the course of a field exercise in West Germany while parked at the roadside. Note the pioneer tools mounted on the sloping hull front and the stowage bin at the rear. Communications are provided by the UK/VRC 353 Clansman radio made by Marconi Space and Defence Systems and common to the entire CVR(T) range. (Pierre Touzin)

64. In another private venture Alvis/USH offer a 'stretched' version of Spartan known as Stormer, which is capable of carrying a complete section of 10–12 infantrymen. With six instead of five wheel stations per side, Stormer is powered by the Perkins T6.3544 diesel engine and it can mount a variety of turrets. In late 1981 the Malaysian Army ordered 25 Stormer APCs, twelve of which are armed with a 20mm Oerlikon cannon in a Helio FVT 900 turret, together with 26 examples of the Scorpion 90, a version mounting a 90mm Cockerill Mk. III gun. The Stormer shown here has firing ports in the sides. (Author)

65. As its name suggests, Samaritan is the armoured ambulance variant of the CVR(T) range. This model has the same hull configuration as the Sultan command vehicle. In accordance with the Geneva Convention, Samaritan displays prominent red crosses and is unarmed. This prototype vehicle is undergoing trials at MVEE in Surrey.

66. Samaritan usually has a crew of two in peacetime – a driver and commander/medical orderly – but in war a second RAMC crewman would be carried. The vehicle is fitted with an air-conditioning unit for the casualty compartment; it is the only variant with this facility for use in North-West Europe.

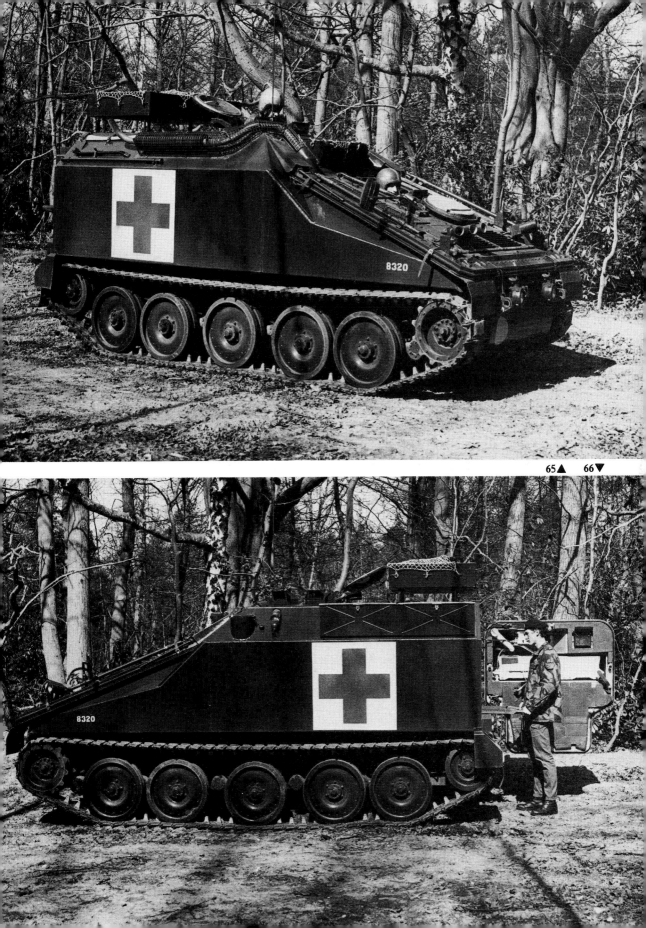

▲67

▼68

67. A prototype
Samaritan bearing the
insignia of the ATDU
(Armoured Trials and
Development Unit)
displays the sort of cross-
country performance
which ensures rapid
casualty evacuation
within armoured units
irrespective of the
terrain over which they
operate.

68. A Samaritan of the
17th/21st Lancers takes
part in Exercise 'Arctic
Express' with the ACE
Mobile Force (Land) to
protect the northern
flank of NATO, the
Lancers acting in the
role of Force Reconnais-
sance Unit. Note the in-
signia of the Lancers and
AMF(L) on either side
of the large red cross.

69. A 'casualty' is treated beside a Samaritan during an exercise. The vehicle can carry four stretcher cases, or five sitting casualties, or two stretcher and three sitting casualties. The two stretchers are to the right, with a bench seat for three 'walking wounded' on the left. (Author)

70. Operating under NBC conditions, an FV104 Samaritan armoured ambulance moves at speed. On the roof is a large stowage container for medical stores, and above each of the red crosses is a rolled-up curtain which can obscure the prominent markings should the vehicle be used in a different role. (Author)

▲ 72 ▼ 73

42

71. (Previous spread) Sultan is the armoured command vehicle of the CVR(T) range. This view of a prototype shows the raised superstructure which gives extra headroom inside for a formation commander and staff officers plus additional internal stowage space for more radios, batteries and mapboards.
72. The prototype Sultan had a superstructure similar to an enlarged Spartan APC, with sloping sides to the roof line. It was designed to replace the FV604 and FV610 Saracen command vehicles which, being wheeled, lacked the full cross-country mobility essential to the conduct of modern armoured warfare.
73. Sultan is used to command armoured, artillery or mechanized infantry units at regimental or squadron/company level. The armament consists of a single pintle-mounted 7.62mm GPMG at the commander's No. 27 cupola, which has five periscopes for all-round

observation plus a single wide-angle periscope with an interchangeable passive night sight.
74. The first production FV105 Sultan was delivered to the British Army in April 1977. Here a Sultan of 1st Royal Tank Regiment moves off during an exercise in West Germany. It carries a crew of up to six men: driver, vehicle commander/radio operator, another radio operator and two or three others of the command staff.
75. The vehicle is equipped to operate four radio nets (note the requisite number of antennae on this Sultan of the 17th/21st Lancers) but two are common, one forwards and one rearwards. Clansman radios are currently fitted, and there is sufficient battery capacity to run the radios and the internal vehicle lighting (plus the essential boiling vessel for endless cups of tea!) for ten hours without recharging. (Author)

▲76   ▼77

76. To increase the amount of working space for the command staff, a penthouse extension can be erected at the rear of the vehicle. A 12m elevating radio antenna for increased range in the static role can also be erected on the sloping hull front. Both items are stowed on the vehicle and are shown to advantage in the photograph. (Author)

77. Sultan shares the same hull configuration as Samaritan, with an additional 12in of headroom in the rear compartment. Sultan provides a formation commander with both armoured protection and mobility on the battlefield and gives him the ability to maintain communications with his troops and with higher headquarters. (Author)

78. An FV105 Sultan Armoured Command Vehicle fulfils its role during an exercise. (Author)

79. Manned by REME personnel, an FV106 Armoured Recovery Vehicle moves off to its next assignment. (Author)

▲81 ▼82

80. (Previous spread) The turret crew of an FV721 CVR(W) Fox discuss their role as pathfinders for a battle-group night march. (Author)

81. Festooned with extra stowage, an FV107 Scimitar Reconnaissance Vehicle pauses before continuing in its recce tasks. (Author)

82. Another private venture by Alvis/USH is the Stormer air defence variant, which is fitted with a General Electric turret mounting a 25mm Gatling gun and a Stinger air defence twin-missile launcher on top. (Author)

83. Samson is the armoured recovery vehicle deployed by the various units using the CVR(T) range. It is manned by members of the Royal Electrical and Mechanical Engineers (REME). The armament consists of a single GPMG and smoke dischargers.

84. The recovery winch and cable drum are mounted in the rear hull compartment and driven from a power take-off on the main engine. The winch is provided with 750ft of wire rope and has a variable speed of up to 400ft a minute. A spade anchor is fitted at the rear to aid stability during recovery operations.

83▲   84▼

49

▲85

85. This three-quarter rear view of the first Samson prototype (00SP38) shows the winch cable passing through an opening beneath the rear door. This configuration proved unsatisfactory and on production vehicles it leads out over the top of the hull at the rear.

▼86

86. Prototype 03SP38 was completed in the early 1970s but as a result of trials extensive redesign work was necessary and Samson did not enter service with the British Army until 1978. As with all vehicles in the CVR(T) range, Samson is fitted with an NBC pack for operation in contaminated conditions.

87. FV106 Samson is fitted with a comprehensive range of tools to recover stranded vehicles, including Marlow kinetic energy tow ropes and a tow bar (seen here stowed on the hull side). The tow bar doubles as an A-frame jib when erected at the rear and used in conjunction with the winch, enabling the Samson to lift and change major assemblies in the field. (Author)

88. Aptly named, Samson perches in mid-air on its rear spade anchors as it recovers a heavily bogged vehicle. The maximum pull with a 4 to 1 snatch block and tackle is 12 tons – sufficient to recover all vehicles in the CVR(T) range as well as heavier ones such as the FV432 APC.

▲89

89. The first prototype of the Scimitar was completed in July 1971 and it was accepted for service with the British Army in June 1973. Scimitar is very similar to Scorpion except that it carries a 30mm Rarden semi-automatic gun instead of the 76mm.

90. This variant has been designed for close reconnaissance. The Rarden gun obtains its name from RARDE (Royal Armament Research and Development Establishment) and Enfield, the former Royal Small Arms Factory, who jointly were responsible for its design.

91. At 17,200lb, Scimitar is the lightest vehicle in the CVR(T) range and has outstanding cross-country mobility which, combined with its low silhouette and compact size, makes it ideally suited to its role of close reconnaissance. (Author)

92. The first production Scimitar was issued to the British Army in March 1974 and the first deliveries to the Belgian Army were made the following month. Typical of CVR(T) in the field, this Scimitar has extensive external stowage with boxes of compo rations strapped to the side beneath the exhaust pipe. (Pierre Touzin)

▼90

▲94

93. (Previous spread) A prototype Scimitar undergoes trials at MVEE, Chertsey. The Rarden gun is very accurate out to ranges in excess of 1km and is particularly effective against hostile APCs and other lightly armoured AFVs.

94. Like Scorpion, Scimitar has a crew of three (here shown in NBC rig, or 'Noddy suits'), comprising driver, gunner and commander/loader. Sighting equipment includes the commander's AV No. 75, the gunner's AV No. 52 and, beside the main armament, an AV 11 No. 43A1 passive night sight.

95. Scimitars of the Queen's Royal Irish Hussars, the Close Reconnaissance Troop of ACE Mobile Force (Land), leaguer in a pine forest during an exercise in Norway.

96. A Scimitar of the 7th Armoured Brigade lies concealed in a wood during Exercise 'Grosser Bär' in Lower Saxony, West Germany. The Rarden gun has a maximum elevation of 35 degrees, which gives it a limited capability against attack helicopters and slow-moving aircraft.

▼95   96▶

▲97 ▼98

97. A Scimitar displays its high acceleration during a mobility demonstration at Bovington. The vehicle is amphibious by means of the flotation screen mounted around the hull. (Author)

98. Adopting a good observation position at the edge of a wood, a Scimitar takes part in Exercise 'Bold Guard' in West Germany. Note the driver's respirator haversack next to his hatch and also the coaxial machine gun.

99. Follwed by an FV432 APC, an FV107 Scimitar moves through a German town during Exercise 'Spearpoint 76'. During the Falklands War a Scimitar of The Blues and Royals was credited with hitting an Argentine Skyhawk jet with its 30mm Rarden gun.

100. A Scimitar of the 9th/12th Royal Lancers (Prince of Wales's) fires its main armament on the Bergen Hohne NATO ranges. Note the empty shell cases on the ground; after firing they are automatically ejected outside the vehicle through a port in the mantlet so that the turret is not cluttered with empty cases or filled with powder fumes.

99▲   100▼

103▲

101. A Scimitar of the 1st Royal Tank Regiment takes to the air as it speeds along a track at the British Army's training area at Suffield, Alberta, in Canada. The flag denotes that it is carrying live ammunition.

102. A convoy of Scimitars of the QRIH takes part in Exercise 'Anorak Express' in Norway during 1981. The Rarden fires four types of ammunition – Armour Piercing Special Effects (APSE), Armour-Piercing Discarding Sabot (APDS), HE and practice rounds. Maximum range for all is about 2km.

103. Masked with foliage, a Scimitar of the 16th/5th Lancers patrols along the Inner German Border during Exercise 'Full House'. The 30mm APSE round is particularly effective against the armour of APCs, MICVs or light AFVs, piercing it and then exploding inside to cause maximum damage to personnel and equipment.

104. A Scimitar negotiates a muddy stream at speed during an exercise in West Germany. With the APDS, similar in design to the highly successful 105mm and 120mm ammunition, any light AFV can be destroyed and the round also has an effective performance against the side and rear armour of main battle tanks.

104▼

▲105 ▼106   107 ▶

105. One hundred and sixty-five rounds of ammunition in clips of three are carried by Scimitar. The Rarden gun can be fired single shot or in bursts of up to six rounds, at a cyclic rate of 80 rounds per minute. The coaxial machine gun carries 3,000 rounds of 7.62mm ammunition.
106. With a Gazelle helicopter hovering in the background, a Scimitar of 'C' Squadron, The Life Guards, undertakes its reconnaissance role during Exercise 'Hardfall' in Norway in 1973.
107. Emerging from a pall of smoke, a Scimitar of the 17th/21st Lancers participates in an exercise in Belize (formerly British Honduras) where a squadron of CVR(T)s is stationed in support of the indigenous army.

108. A Scimitar of the 13th/18th Hussars moves through a wood during an exercise in West Germany. Its compact dimensions enable the vehicle to negotiate such difficult terrain with ease.

109. The author tries his hand at the controls of a Scimitar during a presentation of the CVR(T) range. For a tracked vehicle, CVR(T) is simple to drive and fight – factors that have made the series attractive to foreign armies whose users are lacking the full capabilities to operate sophisticated MBTs. (Author)

110. Designed at the Military Vehicle and Engineering Establishment, Chertsey, and produced at the Royal Ordnance Factory, Leeds, Fox is a logical development of the highly successful Ferret Scout Car.

111. (Next spread) Fox is equipped with a 30mm Rarden gun, a 7.62mm GPMG, smoke dischargers and day and night fighting and vision instruments. Fox is extremely manoeuvrable and, thanks to its high power-to-weight ratio, has excellent cross-country mobility. Here, a prototype goes through its paces at MVEE.

▲108 ▼109

110▶

▲112 ▼113

112. As a companion vehicle to Fox, the FV222 CVR(W)L Vixen was designed as a replacement for the liaison variant of the Ferret Scout Car but incorporating full armour protection and an enclosed machine gun turret.

113. Constructed of aluminium alloy and automotively identical to Fox, Vixen was to be used by all arms, with a crew of two and space for two passengers. It was cancelled in the defence cuts of 1974.

114. Development of the Fox began in 1965, and fifteen prototype vehicles were built by Daimler of Coventry, the manufacturers of Ferret, between November 1967 and April 1969. User trials began in 1968, and the Fox was accepted for service with the British Army in 1970.

115. Fox has a crew of three – a driver, a commander/loader and a gunner/radio operator. The turret carries both main and secondary armament, and the layout is designed so that one man can operate all installed equipment in an emergency.

116. Production began at ROF Leeds in 1972, and the first FV721 Combat Vehicle Reconnaissance (Wheeled) was completed in May 1973. Fox is used by both regular and reserve (Territorial Army) units of the British Army.

114▲

115▲ 116▼

▲117

117. As with CVR(T), Fox uses the militarized XJ Jaguar engine for ease of logistical support, giving the very high power-to-weight ratio of 32bhp/ton and a top speed of 65mph. Four-wheel drive and power steering is standard, affording ease of control and reducing driver fatigue.

118. For its size and weight, Fox has an exceptionally powerful main armament – the Rarden 30mm cannon, as fitted to Scimitar; it is seen here firing on the ranges at Lulworth. With an elevation

range of +40° to −14°, the weapon also has a deterrent capability against slow, low-flying aircraft and helicopters. (Author)

119. Fox armoured cars undergo routine maintenance during an exercise in Germany. By the use of such a well-proven engine and auxiliaries, which are mounted to facilitate withdrawal as a complete power-pack, Fox is highly reliable, and major servicing is necessary only every 5,000 miles or twelve months.

▼118

120. Manned by members of the Royal Hussars, a Fox conducts training on Salisbury Plain. In British Army service, standard equipment includes two radios, night sights and a navigational aid. The flotation screen for amphibious operation has been removed.
121. Apart from armed reconnaissance, Fox can be used for tasks such as patrolling, providing escorts and undertaking internal security duties. In the last-mentioned role, the Fox has been employed in Northern Ireland (as shown here), driver training being conducted by 2nd Royal Tank Regiment in Omagh.

 ▲120 ▼121